INSTANT HAWAIIAN
By
Chris Christensen

Co-Edited
By

Kalani Meinecke
Assistant Professor of Hawaiian
and Anthropology
University of Hawai'i at Hilo

And

Robert Boom

Instant Hawaiian

First Printing, September 1967
18th Printing, Revised Edition, October 1974
21st Printing, Third Edition, March 1976
26th Printing, New Revised Edition, October 1978

BOB BOOM BOOKS

BOX 1922, HILO BAY
HAWAI'I ISLAND, USA 96720

Contents

When looking for a specific word, bear in mind that all terms are listed according to categories. Use the above list to find the group in which the word you seek is most likely to appear. The final section contains an alphabetical listing of Hawaiian terms not included elsewhere in the booklet.

Introduction

So you'd like to learn to speak Hawaiian — you should live so long!

Most people think the Hawaiian Language is a primitive kind of communication that can express only a few primary ideas. Far from it! The most definitive Hawaiian Dictionary contains over 26,000 entries, including many unique terms which reflect the picturesque history, culture, and geography of Hawai'i. For instance, there are 33 ways to indicate a cloud, depending upon the particular kind of cloud you mean. A complete Hawaiian vocabulary lists 179 terms about sweet potatoes alone — and 225 words about the taro plant from which poi is made!

Hence, this Instant Hawaiian word guide is by no means a complete vocabulary. It is, rather, an introduction to terms in common usage by seasoned residents of Hawai'i, designed to help you recognize — both by sight and sound — key expressions which are apt to occur most frequently during everyday conversations in the 50th State.

In recent years a number of Hawaiian words have been making their way into English. By now *Webster's Third New International Dictionary* includes about 125 terms from Hawaiian. This booklet contains many times over that number, and you can learn to use them all with accuracy if you'll spend only a few minutes on every section.

The pronunciation rules on the following pages are simple but important. Become familiar with them, step by step — reviewing occasionally — and you'll soon prove to yourself and your friends how surprisingly easy it is to say all these hundreds of words, correctly and naturally, as though Hawaiian were your second tongue!

A Dozen Letters

The Hawaiian Language has the shortest alphabet in the world. There are only twelve letters—less than half the number you must juggle in English. Five of these are the old familiar vowels: **a, e, i, o, u.** Seven are consonants: **h, k, l, m, n, p, w.**

Hawaiian consonants won't cause you any trouble because they have the same sound as in English. So when you come across **h, k, l, m, n, p, w** — you pronounce them exactly the same as always, with one exception. Occasionally **w** is sounded as **v.** Precisely when it is correct to switch from the **w**-sound to the **v**-sound has become the subject of a great deal of unnecessary confusion.

HERE'S THE HARD AND FAST RULE:

- When the **w** follows the vowels **o** or **u,** the standard **w**-sound is pronounced.

- But when the **w** follows **e** or **i,** it gives way to a **v**-sound.

- If the **w** follows the **a**-vowel, or if the **w** is the first letter in the word, you may suit yourself and pronounce either the **w**-like or **v**-like sound. (The optional **w/v** usage sometimes involves a native preference so all the sound patterns given in this book indicate the traditional choice of Hawaiian speakers.)

BASIC VOWEL SOUNDS

a .... "*uh*" .... as the **a** in **above**
(usually in unstressed syllables)

"*ah*" .... as the **a** in **father**
(usually in stressed syllables,
and when marked Ā or ā)

e .... "*eh*" .... as the **e** in **bed**
(generally kept soft)

"*ay*" .... as the **e** in **they**
(when marked Ē or ē)

i .... "*ee*" .... as the **i** in **police**

o .... "*oh*" .... as the **o** in **vote**

u .... "*oo*" .... as the **u** in **true**

There are fine variations in some of these basic vowel sounds which are known to native speakers and scholars of the language. But persons who are unaccustomed to conversational Hawaiian can use the primary sounds above, and you'll do very well.

THE MACRON

In some words the vowel sounds are held for a longer duration than those above. These "long vowels" are shown in Hawaiian spelling by a bar over the letter:

ā, ē, ī, ō, ū

The bar is called a **macron,** and whenever you see this mārk in a word, be sure to give that vowel a bit more emphasis. Never ignore a macron! Unfortunately, much of the Hawaiian commonly seen in print fails to include this important mark. Without macrons the spelling is incomplete and misleading, and correct pronunciation is impossible.

8

Break It up!

At first glance some Hawaiian terms seem long and difficult. Break these words into syllables and you'll find them easier to say.

Hawaiian syllables never contain more than one consonant — h,k,l,m,n,p,w. For instance, the word "hula" (a native dance telling a story) can't be divided *hul-a*, but is correctly divided *hu-la*.

Whenever you see a consonant, be alerted that it's the beginning of a separately pronounced syllable.

To make things even easier, each syllable must end with a vowel — a,e,i,o,u. Hence, every word in the Hawaiian Language always ends with a vowel. Also, a single vowel can stand alone as a syllable.

Get into the habit of seeing all long words by short syllables. To start, say each syllable slowly and individually — sounding every letter. Let's hear you breeze through the name of this little fish:

humuhumunukunuku'āpua'a

hu|mu|hu|mu|nu|ku|nu|ku|'ā|pu|a|'a

But what was that mark doing back there near the tail end of our little fish? It's not an apostrophe. It's exactly the same as a single opening quotation mark. This is called a **glottal stop** which indicates a total break in sound. Whenever you see one (') cut off all sound for an instant, making an abrupt stop as if your voice gave out momentarily — like the quick pause in the middle of the English expression "Oh-oh!" Then go right on.

Don't be afraid of the glottal stop (called **'u'ina** in Hawaiian) even though we don't have anything like it in English. Some Hawaiian words have more than one glottal stop, and often they occur at the beginning of a word.

It's easy to make these quick glottal stops — and they're important.

The Eight Vowel Pairs

By far the most common type of syllable in Hawaiian consists of one consonant followed by one vowel. Let's put together some simple words. Taking the **ā**-vowel as our basis, we can precede it with the seven consonants — h,k,l,m,n,p,w — and make seven different words:

hā	*"HAH"*	exhalation
kā	*"KAH"*	a vine
lā	*"LAH"*	sun, day
mā	*"MAH"*	discolored
nā	*"NAH"*	calm
pā	*"PAH"*	enclosure
wā	*"WAH"*	roar

What would happen if we added an **e**-vowel to each of the above words? Well, adding another vowel, of course, would change both the sound and meaning of every word. But we wouldn't necessarily get another syllable to pronounce because certain pairs of vowels are pronounced with a gliding lilt, as one syllable. These vowel combinations are: **ae, ai, ao, au, ei, eu, oi, ou.** And here's how it works:

hae	*"HAH⁀eh"*	flag
kae	*"KAH⁀eh"*	scorn
lae	*"LAH⁀eh"*	promontory
mae	*"MAH⁀eh"*	wither
nae	*"NAH⁀eh"*	asthma
pae	*"PAH⁀eh"*	cluster
wae	*"WAH⁀eh"*	choice

Thus words containing any of the eight vowel pairs — **ae, ai, ao, au, ei, eu, oi, ou** — never would be said according to the general practice of sounding every letter individually. Instead, these vowel pairs are merged into one smooth sound, with the first vowel receiving stress.

ae = "**AH**⌣eh"	**ei** = "**EH**⌣ee"
ai = "**AH**⌣ee"	**eu** = "**EH**⌣oo"
ao = "**AH**⌣oh"	**oi** = "**OH**⌣ee"
au = "**AH**⌣oo"	**ou** = "**OH**⌣oo"

Be sure to learn these eight vowel pairs so every time you see them you'll remember to "link⌣together" and not sound each vowel equally.

Hawaiian vowel pairs are not as closely joined in pronunciation as the dipthongs in English.

au = "**AH**⌣oo"................not: "OW"
lei = "**LEH**⌣ee"..............not: "LAY"
poi = "**POH**⌣ee".............not: "POY"

Stress in Pronunciation

And now we find ourselves face to face with the problem of pronouncing Hawaiian words of more than one syllable.

Once we have broken a word into its basic sound pattern, naturally, we don't say every syllable with equal stress. Such a practice would produce a dull monotone and we'd lose the rhythm and beauty of the language. So we must learn to place our emphasis.

In Hawaiian the main accent of a word usually falls on the *next-to-the-last* syllable. Therefore, in words of only two syllables, the first half generally is stressed:

lio   *LEE*-oh   horse

Words of three syllables also receive their stress on the *next-to-the-last* syllable:

koloa   *koh-LOH-uh*   wild duck

Words of more than three syllables receive slight additional stress on *every-other* preceding syllable. This sets up a pleasant, alternating pattern of sound:

malihini   *MAH-lee-HEE-nee*   newcomer

The main exception to the above pattern of stress is the five syllable word which takes two accents of equal strength on the first and fourth syllables. You will not encounter this deviation often because there are only a few "pure" five syllable words in the Hawaiian Language.

ānuenue   *AH-noo-eh-NOO-eh*   rainbow

Hawaiian terms with three or more syllables are often compound words. Examples of compound words in English are: **surfboard, motorboat, nevertheless.** These longer terms require a basic knowledge of their internal "root words" in order to place accents accurately because each separate word within a compound term needs to be said as an independent unit and smoothly blended with the other parts. Whenever you come across a long Hawaiian word, be sure to check it in the standard references so you can see if you're dealing with a compound word.

The vowel pairs, discussed in the preceding section, always require stress. Any syllable with a vowel pair is emphasized:

makai	*muh-KAH~ee*	seaward
mauka	*MAH~oo-kuh*	inland

When considering which syllable to stress, remember the importance of the **macron: ā,ē,ī,ō,ū.** These marked vowels also require stress:

manoa	*muh-NOH-uh*	many
mānoa	*MAH-NOH-uh*	vast, thick

The presence of macrons in Hawaiian words also can require us to make a "macron shift" in emphasis:

huhu	*HOO-hoo*	wormy
huhū	*hoo-HOO*	angry

Simplification

Have you noticed the frequent repetition within numerous Hawaiian words? Take our little friend **humuhumunukunuku'āpua'a**. It's confusing at first sight, but as you look it over, you'll realize that what you have before you is a kind of verse!

> Humu-humu,
> nuku-nuku,
> 'ā,
> pua'a.

Duplicate spellings not only make it possible to lump similar syllables into groups — they also establish catchy tempos which are helpful in making words stick in the memory. You should have no trouble learning these Hawaiian terms for colors:

ke'oke'o	*KEH-'oh-KEH-'oh*	white
'ele'ele	*'EH-leh-'EH-leh*	black
uliuli	*OO-lee-OO-lee*	dark
'ula'ula	*'OO-luh-'OO-luh*	red
melemele	*MEH-leh-MEH-leh*	yellow
lenalena	*LEH-nuh-LEH-nuh*	pale yellow
'ōma'oma'o	*'OH-MAH-'oh-MAH-'oh*	green
'āhina	*'AH-HEE-nuh*	gray, silver
'alani	*'uh-LAH-nee*	orange
polū	*poh-LOO*	blue
'ākala	*'AH-KAH-luh*	pink
poni	*POH-nee*	purple
palaunu	*puh-LAH⌐oo-noo*	brown
kula	*KOO-luh*	gold

Nature

honua	hoh-**NOO**-uh	earth
ahi	**AH**-hee	fire
wai	**WAH**⁀ee	fresh water
kai	**KAH**⁀ee	sea water
moana	moh-**AH**-nuh	ocean
ānuenue	**AH**-NOO-eh-**NOO**-eh	rainbow
ua	**OO**-uh	rain
lā	**LAH**	sun, day
lani	**LAH**-nee	sky, heaven
mahina	muh-**HEE**-nuh	moon, lunar month
hōkū	**HOH**-**KOO**	star
makani	muh-**KAH**-nee	wind
'ino'ino	'**EE**-noh-'**EE**-noh	storm
uila	oo-**EE**-luh	lightning
hekili	heh-**KEE**-lee	thunder
ao	**AH**⁀oh	daylight, cloud
manu	**MAH**-noo	bird
mauna	**MAH**⁀oo-nuh	mountain
pu'u	**POO**-'oo	hill
lepo	**LEH**-poh	dirt, soil
pōhaku	POH-**HAH**-koo	stone, rock
wailele	WAH⁀ee-**LEH**-leh	waterfall
kahawai	KAH-huh-**WAH**⁀ee	stream
one	**CH**-neh	sand
kahakai	KAH-huh-**KAH**⁀ee	beach
nahele	nuh-**HEH**-leh	forest
lā'au	LAH-'**AH**⁀oo	tree, plant, wood
lau	**LAH**⁀oo	leaf
hua	**HOO**-uh	fruit, seed
pua	**POO**-uh	flower
holoholona	**HOH**-loh-hoh-**LOH**-nuh	animal

16

Times

Now that you're familiar with the basic structure of Hawaiian terms, you'll be seeing more examples of compound words. As your vocabulary increases you'll find yourself able to express more by coining the words you're learning into various combinations.

Remember that in Hawaiian the noun generally comes first and then you add modifiers.

au	*AH⌢oo*	era
kau	*KAH⌢oo*	season
kau wela	*KAH⌢oo WEH⌢luh*	summer
ho'oilo	*HOH-'oh-EE-loh*	winter
makahiki	*MAH-kuh-HEE-kee*	year
lānui	*LAH-NOO-ee*	holiday
keia lā	*KEH⌢ee-uh LAH*	today
'apōpō	*'uh-POH-POH*	tomorrow
nehinei	*NEH-hee-NEH⌢ee*	yesterday
mahina hou	*muh-HEE-nuh HOH⌢oo*	new moon
mahina piha	*muh-HEE-nuh PEE-huh*	full moon
pō mahina	*POH muh-HEE-nuh*	moonlight night
pō	*POH*	night
pō'ele'ele	*POH-'EH-leh-'EH-leh*	darkness
wana'ao	*VAH-nuh-'AH⌢oh*	dawn
pukana lā	*poo-KAH-nuh LAH*	sunrise
mālamalama	*MAH-LAH-muh-LAH-muh*	light
kakahiaka	*kah-KAH-hee-AH-kuh*	morning
awakea	*AH-vuh-KEH-uh*	noon
'auinalā	*'AH⌢oo-ee-nuh-LAH*	afternoon
napo'o lā	*nuh-POH-'oh LAH*	sunset
pōlehulehu	*POH-LEH-hoo-LEH-hoo*	dusk
ahiahi	*AH-hee-AH-hee*	evening
aumoe	*AH⌢oo-MOH-eh*	midnight

Parts of the Body

kino	*KEE*-noh	body
iwi	*EE*-vee	bone
iwi 'ao'ao	*EE*-vee *'AH⌒oh*-*'AH⌒oh*	rib
'i'o	*'EE*-'oh	muscle, flesh
koko	*KOH*-koh	blood
momona	moh-*MOH*-nuh	fat
'ili	*'EE*-lee	skin
lauoho	*LAH⌒oo*-*OH*-hoh	hair
huluhulu	*HOO*-loo-*HOO*-loo	body hair
'umi'umi	*'OO*-mee-*'OO*-mee	beard, mustache
po'o	*POH*-'oh	head
iwi po'o	*EE*-vee *POH*-'oh	skull
lolo	*LOH*-loh	brain
lae	*LAH⌒eh*	forehead
maha	*MAH*-huh	temple
helehelena	*HEH*-leh-heh-*LEH*-nuh	features
papālina	puh-*PAH*-*LEE*-nuh	cheek
pepeiao	peh-*PEH⌒ee*-*AH⌒oh*	ear
maka	*MAH*-kuh	face, eye
lihilihi	*LEE*-hee-*LEE*-hee	eyelashes
ku'eku'emaka	*KOO*-'eh-*KOO*-'eh-*MAH*-kuh	eyebrows
ihu	*EE*-hoo	nose
pukaihu	*POO*-kuh-*EE*-hoo	nostril
waha	*WAH*-huh	mouth
lehelehe	*LEH*-heh-*LEH*-heh	lip
niho	*NEE*-hoh	teeth
alelo	uh-*LEH*-loh	tongue
pu'u	*POO*-'oo	throat
'auwae	*'AH⌒oo*-*WAH⌒eh*	chin
'ā'ī	*'AH*-*'EE*	neck
po'ohiwi	*POH*-'oh-*HEE*-vee	shoulder

18

Hawaiian	Pronunciation	English
lima	**LEE**-muh	arm, hand
ku'eku'e lima	KOO-'eh-**KOO**-'eh **LEE**-muh	elbow
pūlima	POO-**LEE**-muh	wrist
pu'ulima	POO-'oo-**LEE**-muh	fist, knuckles
poho	**POH**-hoh	palm
manamana	MAH-nuh-**MAH**-nuh	finger
manamana lima nui	MAH-nuh-**MAH**-nuh **LEE**-muh **NOO**-ee	thumb
miki'ao	MEE-kee-'**AH**⁀oh	finger/toe nails
umauma	oo-**MAH**⁀oo-muh	chest
poli	**POH**-lee	bosom
pu'uwai	POO-'oo-**WAH**⁀ee	heart
akemāmā	AH-keh-**MAH-MAH**	lung
kua	**KOO**-uh	back
iwikuamo'o	EE-vee-KOO-uh-**MOH**-'oh	spine
kīkala	KEE-**KAH**-luh	hip
pūhaka	POO-**HAH**-kuh	waist
'ōpū	'**OH**-**POO**	stomach
piko	**PEE**-koh	navel
na'au	nuh-'**AH**⁀oo	intestines, bowels
ule	**OO**-leh	penis
kohe	**KOH**-heh	vagina
lemu	**LEH**-moo	buttocks
'ōkole	'**OH**-**KOH**-leh	anus
wāwae	WAH-**WAH**⁀eh	leg, foot
'ūhā	'**OO**-**HAH**	thigh
kuli	**KOO**-lee	knee
ku'eku'e wāwae	KOO-'eh-**KOO**-'eh WAH-**WAH**⁀eh	ankle, heel
manamana wāwae	MAH-nuh-**MAH**-nuh WAH-**WAH**⁀eh	toe

Food

pōloli	*POH-**LOH**-lee*	hungry
'ai	*'**AH**⁓ee*	food, to eat
mea 'ai	*MEH-uh '**AH**⁓ee*	food
pūpū	***POO-POO***	appetizer; shell
kaukau	*KAH⁓oo-**KAH**⁓oo*	"chow" (slang)
lū'au	*LOO-'**AH**⁓oo*	feast
'aina	*'**AH**⁓ee-nuh*	meal
inu	***EE**-noo*	drink
wai	***WAH**⁓ee*	fresh water; liquid
wai niu	***WAH**⁓ee **NEE**-oo*	coconut water
wai momona	***WAH**⁓ee moh-**MOH**-nuh*	punch, soda
waihua'ai	*WAH⁓ee-HOO-uh-'**AH**⁓ee*	fruit juice
waiū	*WAH⁓ee-**OO***	milk
waiūpaka	*WAH⁓ee-OO-**PAH**-kuh*	butter
waiūpakapa'a	*WAH⁓ee-OO-PAH-kuh-**PAH**-'ah*	cheese
kalima	*kuh-**LEE**-muh*	cream
kī	***KEE***	tea
kope	***KOH**-peh*	coffee
pia	***PEE**-uh*	beer
kupa	***KOO**-puh*	soup
pa'akai	*PAH-'uh-**KAH**⁓ee*	salt
kō	***KOH***	sugar cane, sugar
'inamona	*'**EE**-nuh-**MOH**-nuh*	kukui nut relish
pipi	***PEE**-pee*	beef
pipi kaula	***PEE**-pee **KAH**⁓oo-luh*	jerk beef
pua'a	*poo-**AH**-'ah*	pork
pua'a kālua	*poo-**AH**-'ah KAH-**LOO**-uh*	baked pig
moa	***MOH**-uh*	chicken
hua	***HOO**-uh*	egg
kukui haole	*koo-**KOO**-ee **HAH**⁓oh-leh*	nut

i'a	*EE*-'uh	fish
i'a maka	*EE*-'uh *MAH*-kuh	raw fish
mahimahi	*MAH*-hee-*MAH*-hee	dolphin
kamano lomi	kuh-*MAH*-noh *LOH*-mee	salted salmon
'ahi	*'AH*-hee	tuna
'ula	*'OO*-luh	lobster
pāpa'i	PAH-*PAH*-'ee	crab
'ōpae	*'OH*-*PAH*⁓eh	shrimp
'ōlepe	*'OH*-*LEH*-peh	oyster
he'e	*HEH*-'eh	squid, octopus
puhi	*POO*-hee	eel
'ōpihi	*'OH*-*PEE*-hee	limpet
limu	*LEE*-moo	seaweed
laulau	*LAH*⁓oo-*LAH*⁓oo	food wrapped in
		leaves and steamed
kalo	*KAH*-loh	taro
poi	*POH*⁓ee	mashed taro
uhi	*OO*-hee	yam
'uwala	'oo-*WAH*-luh	sweet potato
'ulu	*'OO*-loo	breadfruit
hua'ai	HOO-uh-*'AH*⁓ee	fruit
mai'a	*MAH*⁓ee-'uh	banana
hala kahiki	*HAH*-luh kuh-*HEE*-kee	pineapple
'alani	'uh-*LAH*-nee	orange
ipuhaole	EE-poo-*HAH*⁓oh-leh	watermelon
niu	*NEE*-oo	coconut
haupia	HAH⁓oo-*PEE*-uh	coconut pudding
kūlolo	KOO-*LOH*-loh	taro & coconut
		cream pudding
palaoa	puh-*LAH*⁓oh-uh	bread, flour
laiki	*LAH*⁓ee-kee	rice
mea'ono	*MEH*-uh-*'OH*-noh	cake
haukalima	*HAH*⁓oo-kuh-*LEE*-muh	ice cream

Relationships

akua	uh-**KOO**-uh	God, spirit, idol
mō'ī	**MOH**-'**EE**	king
ali'i	uh-**LEE**-'ee	chief
maka'āinana	MAH-kuh-'**AH**‿ee-**NAH**-nuh	commoner
kauwā	KAH‿oo-**WAH**	outcast, servant
'ohana	'oh-**HAH**-nuh	relative, family
kāne	**KAH**-neh	male, husband
wahine	wuh-**HEE**-neh	female, wife
makua	muh-**KOO**-uh	parent
makuakāne	muh-KOO-uh-**KAH**-neh	father
makuahine	muh-KOO-uh-**HEE**-neh	mother
keiki	**KEH**‿ee-kee	baby, child
keikikāne	**KEH**‿ee-kee-**KAH**-neh	boy, son
kaikamahine	**KAH**‿ee-KAH-muh-**HEE**-neh	girl, daughter
kamali'i	KAH-muh-**LEE**-'ee	children
'anakala	'**AH**-nuh-**KAH**-luh	uncle
'anakē	'**AH**-nuh-**KAY**	aunt
kupuna	koo-**POO**-nuh	grandparent, ancestor
tūtū	**TOO**-**TOO**	granny
mo'opuna	**MOH**-'oh-**POO**-nuh	grandchild
mamo	**MAH**-moh	descendant
kaikunāne	**KAH**‿ee-koo-**NAH**-neh	brother
kaikuahine	**KAH**‿ee-KOO-uh-**HEE**-neh	sister
māhoe	MAH-**HOH**-eh	twin
hoahānau	HOH-uh-HAH-**NAH**‿oo	cousin
makamaka	MAH-kuh-**MAH**-kuh	friend
hoa	**HOH**-uh	companion
hoaloha	HOH-uh-**LOH**-huh	good friend
hoapili	HOH-uh-**PEE**-lee	intimate friend
hoalauna	HOH-uh-**LAH**‿oo-nuh	neighbor

Women's Names in Hawaiian

Hawaiian	Pronunciation	English
Apikalia	*AH*-pee-kuh-*LEE*-uh	Abigail
Aka	*AH*-kuh	Ada
Akeneki	AH-keh-*NEH*-kee	Agnes
Alepeka	AH-leh-*PEH*-kuh	Alberta
Aleka	ah-*LEH*-kuh	Alice
Alema	ah-*LEH*-muh	Alma
Eme	*EH*-meh	Amy
Anakela	AH-nuh-*KEH*-luh	Angela, Angie
Anika	uh-*NEE*-kuh	Anita
Ana	*AH*-nuh	Ann, Anna, Anne
Aneka	uh-*NEH*-kuh	Annette
Ane	*AH*-neh	Annie
Alina	uh-*LEE*-nuh	Arleen
Aukele	AH⁀oo-*KEH*-leh	Audrey
Palapala	*PAH*-luh-*PAH*-luh	Barbara
Peakalika	*PEH*-uh-kuh-*LEE*-kuh	Beatrice
Peke	*PEH*-keh	Becky
Pelenike	*PEH*-leh-*NEE*-keh	Bernice
Peleka	peh-*LEH*-kuh	Bertha
Pakake	puh-*KAH*-keh	Bessie
Peke	*PEH*-keh	Betsy, Betty, Bette
Pēweli	*PAY*-VEH-lee	Beverly
Palaneke	*PAH*-luh-*NEH*-keh	Blanche
Poni	*POH*-nee	Bonnie
Palēnaka	puh-*LAY*-NAH-kuh	Brenda
Pilikika	*PEE*-lee-*KEE*-kuh	Bridget
Kaloka	kuh-*LOH*-kuh	Carlotta
Kalamela	KAH-luh-*MEH*-luh	Carmen
Kālola	*KAH*-LOH-luh	Carol
Kalolaina	KAH-loh-*LAH*⁀ee-nuh	Caroline
Kikīlia	kee-*KEE*-*LEE*-uh	Cecelia, Cecilia

Halaki	*hah-**LAH**-kee*	Charlotte, Sharlot
Kelela	*keh-**LEH**-luh*	Cheryl
Kilikina	*KEE-lee-**KEE**-nuh*	Christina, Christine
Kalea	*kuh-**LEH**-uh*	Claire
Kalala	*kuh-**LAH**-luh*	Clara
Kalaukia	*kuh-LAH⁀oo-**KEE**-uh*	Claudia
Kani	***KAH**-nee*	Connie, Conny
Kinikia	*KEE-nee-**KEE**-uh*	Cynthia
Kaeki	***KAH**⁀eh-kee*	Daisy
Kepola	*keh-**POH**-luh*	Deborah
Kiana	*kee-**AH**-nuh*	Diana, Diane
Kina	***KEE**-nuh*	Dinah
Kololeke	*KOH-loh-**LEH**-keh*	Dolores
Kona	***KOH**-nuh*	Donna
Kola	***KOH**-luh*	Dora
Kolika	*koh-**LEE**-kuh*	Doris
Kōleka	***KOH**-LEH-kuh*	Dorothy
Ekika	*eh-**KEE**-kuh*	Edith
Ekena	*eh-**KEH**-nuh*	Edna
Ailina	*AH⁀ee-**LEE**-nuh*	Eileen
Ileina	*ee-**LEH**⁀ee-nuh*	Elaine, Elayne
Elenola	*EH-leh-**NOH**-loh*	Eleanor, Elinor
Elikapeka	*eh-LEE-kuh-**PEH**-kuh*	Elizabeth
Ela	***EH**-luh*	Ella
Elena	*eh-**LEH**-nuh*	Ellen
Eloika	*eh-**LOH**⁀ee-kuh*	Eloise
Eleki	*eh-**LEH**-kee*	Elsie
Emelē	***EH**-meh-LAY*	Emily, Emilie
Ema	***EH**-muh*	Emma
Elika	*eh-**LEE**-kuh*	Erica, Erika
Ekekela	*eh-keh-**KEH**-luh*	Estelle, Esther
Ekela	*eh-**KEH**-luh*	Ethel
Eunike	*EH⁀oo-**NEE**-keh*	Eunice

24

Iwa	*EE*-vuh	Eve, Eva
Ewalina	*EH*-vuh-*LEE*-nuh	Evelyn
Mana'o'i'o	*MAH*-nuh-'oh-'*EE*-'oh	Faith
Pane	*PAH*-neh	Fannie, Fanny
Pololena	*POH*-loh-*LEH*-nuh	Florence
Palakika	*PAH*-luh-*KEE*-kuh	Frances
Kaila	*KAH*⁀ee-luh	Gail, Gale
Keokia	*KEH*-oh-*KEE*-uh	Georgia
Kekaluka	*KEH*-kuh-*LOO*-kuh	Gertrude
Kalākeke	kuh-*LAH*-*KEH*-keh	Gladis, Gladys
Kololia	*KOH*-loh-*LEE*-uh	Gloria
Kaleki	kuh-*LEH*-kee	Grace
Hana	*HAH*-nuh	Hannah
Haliaka	*HAH*-lee-*AH*-kuh	Harriet
Hakela	huh-*KEH*-luh	Hazel
Helena	heh-*LEH*-nuh	Helen
Heneliaka	*HEH*-neh-lee-*AH*-kuh	Henrietta
Kekala	keh-*KAH*-luh	Hester
Hileka	hee-*LEH*-kuh	Hilda
Mana'olana	*MAH*-nuh-'oh-*LAH*-nuh	Hope
Aika	*AH*⁀ee-kuh	Ida
Inakika	*EE*-nuh-*KEE*-kuh	Ingrid
Ailina	*AH*⁀ee-*LEE*-nuh	Irene
Ikapela	*EE*-kuh-*PEH*-luh	Isabel
Keakalina	*KEH*-ah-kuh-*LEE*-nuh	Jacqueline
Kini	*KEE*-nee	Jane, Jean, Jenny
Ianeke	*EE*-uh-*NEH*-keh	Janet, Janette
Kānike	*KAH*-*NEE*-keh	Janice
Ieke	ee-*EH*-keh	Jessie
Kila	*KEE*-luh	Jill
Iō'ana	ee-*OH*-'*AH*-nuh	Joan, Joanne
Iokepine	*EE*-oh-keh-*PEE*-neh	Josephine
Ioi	ee-*OH*⁀ee	Joy

25

Ioke	ee-**OH**-keh	Joyce
Wanika	wuh-**NEE**-kuh	Juanita
Iuki	ee-**OO**-kee	Judy
Iulia	**EE**-oo-**LEE**-uh	Julia, Julie
Iune	ee-**OO**-neh	June
Kālena	**KAH**-LEH-nuh	Karen
Keke	**KEH**-keh	Kate, Katie
Kakalina	KAH-kuh-**LEE**-nuh	Katherine
Kakaline	KAH-kuh-**LEE**-neh	Kathleen
Kei	**KEH**⁀ee	Kay, Kaye
Lala	**LAH**-luh	Laura
Leonola	LEH-oh-**NOH**-luh	Leonora
Lipi	**LEE**-pee	Libby
Līnaka	**LEE**-NAH-kuh	Linda
Liliana	LEE-lee-**AH**-nuh	Lillian
Lilia	lee-**LEE**-uh	Lily, Lilly
Loika	loh-**EE**-kuh	Lois
Loleka	loh-**LEH**-kuh	Loretta
Loleina	loh-**LEH**⁀ee-nuh	Lorraine
Luika	loo-**EE**-kuh	Louisa, Louise
Lukila	loo-**KEE**-luh	Lucille
Luke	**LOO**-keh	Lucy
Lukia	loo-**KEE**-uh	Lydia
Lina	**LEE**-nuh	Lynn
Meipala	MEH⁀ee-**PAH**-luh	Mabel
Makelina	MAH-keh-**LEE**-nuh	Madeline
Malakia	MAH-luh-**KEE**-uh	Marcia
Makaleka	MAH-kuh-**LEH**-kuh	Margaret
Meleana	MEH-leh-**AH**-nuh	Marianne, Marion
Malaea	muh-**LAH**⁀eh-uh	Maria
Malia	muh-**LEE**-uh	Marie
Melelina	MEH-leh-**LEE**-nuh	Marilyn
Makoli	muh-**KOH**-lee	Marjorie

26

Malina	*muh-**LEE**-nuh*	Marlene
Māleka	***MAH**-LEH-kuh*	Marsha, Martha
Malia	*muh-**LEE**-uh*	Mary
Mei	***MEH**~ee*	May, Mae
Mikala	*mee-**KAH**-luh*	Michael, Michelle
Milikeleka	***MEE**-lee-keh-**LEH**-kuh*	Mildred
Mile	***MEE**-leh*	Millie, Milly
Mine	***MEE**-neh*	Minnie
Miliama	***MEE**-lee-**AH**-muh*	Miriam
Miuliela	***MEE**-oo-lee-**EH**-luh*	Muriel
Milena	*mee-**LEH**-nuh*	Myrna
Makala	*muh-**KAH**-luh*	Myrtle
Naneki	*nuh-**NEH**-kee*	Nancy
Nakeli	*nuh-**KEH**-lee*	Natalie
Nele	***NEH**-leh*	Nell, Nellie
Nolina	*noh-**LEE**-nuh*	Noreen
Noma	***NOH**-muh*	Norma
Oleka	*oh-**LEH**-kuh*	Olga
Oliwa	*oh-**LEE**-vuh*	Olive
Olīwia	*oh-LEE-**VEE**-uh*	Olivia
Pāmila	***PAH**-MEE-luh*	Pamela
Pakelekia	*puh-**KEH**-leh-**KEE**-uh*	Patricia
Poleke	*poh-**LEH**-keh*	Paulette
Polina	*poh-**LEE**-nuh*	Pauline
Momi	***MOH**-mee*	Pearl
Peki	***PEH**-kee*	Peggy
Peni	***PEH**-nee*	Penny
Piliki	*pee-**LEE**-kee*	Phyllis
Pole	***POH**-leh*	Polly
Pelekila	*PEH-leh-**KEE**-luh*	Priscilla
Lāhela	***LAH**-HEH-luh*	Rachel
Lamona	*luh-**MOH**-nuh*	Ramona
Lepeka	*leh-**PEH**-kuh*	Rebecca

Hawaiian	Pronunciation	English
Lopeka	loh-**PEH**-kuh	Roberta
Lōpine	**LOH**-PEE-neh	Robin
Lōkālia	LOH-KAH-**LEE**-uh	Rosalie
Loke	**LOH**-keh	Rose
Lokemele	LOH-keh-**MEH**-leh	Rosemary
Lokana	loh-**KAH**-nuh	Roxanna, Roxane
Lupe	**LOO**-peh	Ruby
Luka	**LOO**-kuh	Ruth
Kale	**KAH**-leh	Sally
Kānela	**KAH**-NEH-luh	Sandra
Kala	**KAH**-luh	Sara, Sarah
Kālona	**KAH**-LOH-nuh	Sharon
Kaila	**KAH**⁓ee-luh	Sheila, Shelagh
Kele	**KEH**-leh	Shirley
Kopia	koh-**PEE**-uh	Sophia
Kekepania	**KEH**-keh-puh-**NEE**-uh	Stephanie
Kukana	koo-**KAH**-nuh	Susan, Susannah
Kuke	**KOO**-keh	Susie
Kiliwia	KEE-lee-**VEE**-uh	Sylvia, Cylvia
Kama	**KAH**-muh	Thelma
Keleka	keh-**LEH**-kuh	Theresa, Teresa
Wālelia	VAH-leh-**LEE**-uh	Valerie, Valery
Wila	**VEE**-luh	Vera
Wiki	**VEE**-kee	Vicky
Wikōlia	vee-**KOH**-LEE-uh	Victoria
Waiola	VAH⁓ee-**OH**-luh	Viola
Waioleka	VAH⁓ee-oh-**LEH**-kuh	Violet
Wilikīnia	VEE-lee-**KEE**-NEE-uh	Virginia
Wiwiana	VEE-vee-**AH**-nuh	Vivian
Wanaka	wah-**NAH**-kuh	Wanda
Wilima	wee-**LEE**-muh	Wilma
Winipeleke	**WEE**-nee-peh-**LEH**-keh	Winifred
Iwone	ee-**VOH**-neh	Yvonne

28

Men's Names in Hawaiian

Akamu	ah-**KAH**-moo	Adam
Alena	ah-**LEH**-nuh	Alan, Allen
Alapake	AH-luh-**PAH**-keh	Albert
Alika	ah-**LEE**-kuh	Alec, Alexander
Alapai	AH-luh-**PAH**⌢ee	Alfred
Alewina	AH-leh-**VEE**-nuh	Alvin
Analū	AH-nuh-**LOO**	Andrew
Akoni	ah-**KOH**-nee	Anthony
Ake	**AH**-keh	Archie, Archibald
Aka	**AH**-kuh	Arthur
Peni	**PEH**-neh	Ben
Peniamina	**PEH**-nee-uh-**MEE**-nuh	Benjamin
Pelenalako	**PEH**-leh-nuh-**LAH**-koh	Bernard
Peka	**PEH**-kuh	Bert, Burt
Pila	**PEE**-luh	Bill
Lopaka	loh-**PAH**-kuh	Bob
Palaina	puh-**LAH**⌢ee-nuh	Brian, Bryan
Puluke	poo-**LOO**-keh	Bruce
Kalawina	KAH-luh-**VEE**-nuh	Calvin
Kala	**KAH**-luh	Carl, Karl
Kekila	keh-**KEE**-luh	Cecil
Kale	**KAH**-leh	Charles
Kilikikopa	**KEE**-lee-kee-**KOH**-puh	Christopher
Kalalena	KAH-luh-**LEH**-nuh	Clarence
Kaela	**KAH**⌢eh-luh	Dale
Kana	**KAH**-nuh	Dan, Dana
Kanaiela	kuh-NAH⌢ee-**EH**-luh	Daniel
Kāwika	**KAH**-VEE-kuh	David
Kenika	keh-**NEE**-kuh	Dennis
Likeke	lee-**KEH**-keh	Dick
Kona	**KOH**-nuh	Don

Konala	*koh-NAH-luh*	Donald
Koukalaka	*KOH~oo-kuh-LAH-kuh*	Douglas
Kuaika	*koo-AH~ee-kuh*	Dwight
Ele	*EH-leh*	Earl, Earle
Ekeka	*eh-KEH-kuh*	Edgar
Ekemona	*EH-keh-MOH-nuh*	Edmond
Ekewaka	*EH-keh-WAH-kuh*	Edward
Eluene	*EH-loo-EH-neh*	Edwin
Elema	*eh-LEH-muh*	Elmer
Elika	*eh-LEE-kuh*	Eric, Erik
Eleneki	*EH-leh-NEH-kee*	Ernest
Iukini	*EE-oo-KEE-nee*	Eugene
Poloika	*poh-LOH~ee-kuh*	Floyd
Palakiko	*PAH-luh-KEE-koh*	Francis
Palani	*puh-LAH-nee*	Frank
Peleke	*peh-LEH-keh*	Fred
Kali	*KAH-lee*	Gary
Kini	*KEE-nee*	Gene
Keoki	*keh-OH-kee*	George
Kelala	*keh-LAH-luh*	Gerald
Kilipaki	*KEE-lee-PAH-kee*	Gilbert
Kelena	*keh-LEH-nuh*	Glenn
Kolekona	*KOH-leh-KOH-nuh*	Gordon
Kelekolio	*keh-LEH-koh-LEE-oh*	Gregory
Haneke	*hah-NEH-keh*	Hank, Hans
Halola	*hah-LOH-luh*	Harold
Hale	*HAH-leh*	Harry
Halewe	*hah-LEH-veh*	Harvey
Hanalē	*HAH-nuh-LAY*	Henry
Hapaki	*hah-PAH-kee*	Herbert
Helemano	*HEH-leh-MAH-noh*	Herman
Haoa	*HAH~oo-uh*	Howard
Hupeka	*hoo-PEH-kuh*	Hubert

Hiu	*HEE*-oo	Hugh
Keaka	keh-*AH*-kuh	Jack, Jacques
Kimo	*KEE*-moh	James, Jim
Kē	*KAY*	Jay
Keopele	KEH-oh-*PEH*-leh	Jeffrey, Geoffrey
Ielome	EE-eh-*LOH*-meh	Jerome
Kele	*KEH*-leh	Jerry
Keō	keh-*OH*	Joe
Keoni	keh-*OH*-nee	John, Jon
Ionakana	EE-oh-nuh-*KAH*-nuh	Jonathan
Iokepa	EE-oh-*KEH*-puh	Joseph
Kika	*KEE*-kuh	Keith
Keneke	keh-*NEH*-keh	Kenneth
Lauleneke	*LAH*⁓oo-leh-*NEH*-keh	Lawrence
Lio	*LEE*-oh	Leo
Leonaka	LEH-oh-*NAH*-kuh	Leonard
Loeka	loh-*EH*-kuh	Lloyd
Lui	*LOO*-ee	Louis, Lewis
Malakoma	MAH-luh-*KOH*-muh	Malcolm
Maleko	mah-*LEH*-koh	Marc, Mark
Makini	mah-*KEE*-nee	Martin
Makaio	mah-*KAH*⁓ee-oh	Matthew
Melewina	MAH-leh-*VEE*-nuh	Melvin
Mikaʻele	MEE-kuh-*ʻEH*-leh	Michael, Mike
Neki	*NEH*-kee	Ned
Nikolao	NEE-koh-*LAH*⁓oh	Nicholas
Noela	noh-*EH*-luh	Noel
Nōmana	*NOH*-MAH-nuh	Norman
Oliwa	oh-*LEE*-vuh	Oliver
Oka	*OH*-kuh	Oscar
Okewoleka	OH-keh-woh-*LEH*-kuh	Oswald
Oko	*OH*-koh	Otto
Owene	oh-*WEH*-neh	Owen

Pakelika	*PAH-keh-**LEE**-kuh*	Patrick
Paulo	***PAH**~oo-loh*	Paul
Pekelo	*peh-**KEH**-loh*	Peter
Pilipo	*pee-**LEE**-poh*	Philip
Lalepa	*lah-**LEH**-puh*	Ralph
Lei	***LEH**~ee*	Ray
Leimana	***LEH**~ee-MAH-nuh*	Raymond
Leke	***LEH**-keh*	Rex
Likeke	*lee-**KEH**-keh*	Richard
Lopaka	*loh-**PAH**-kuh*	Robert
Lopine	*loh-**PEE**-neh*	Robin
Lokenē	*LOH-keh-**NAY***	Rodney
Lōkela	***LOH**-KEH-luh*	Roger
Lolana	*loh-**LAH**-nuh*	Roland
Lonala	*loh-**NAH**-luh*	Ronald
Loe	***LOH**-eh*	Roy
Lūkela	***LOO**-KEH-luh*	Russell
Kamuela	*KAH-moo-**EH**-luh*	Samuel
Koka	***KOH**-kuh*	Scott
Kikinē	*KEE-kee-**NAY***	Sidney
Kanalē	*KAH-nuh-**LAY***	Stanley
Kiwini	*kee-**VEE**-nee*	Stephen, Steven
Keli	***KEH**-lee*	Terry
Keokolo	*KEH-oh-**KOH**-loh*	Theodore, Ted
Kimokeo	*KEE-moh-**KEH**-oh*	Timothy
Koma	***KOH**-muh*	Thomas, Tom
Wenona	*veh-**NOH**-nuh*	Vernon
Wikoli	*vee-**KOH**-lee*	Victor
Walaka	*wah-**LAH**-kuh*	Walter
Walena	*wah-**LEH**-nuh*	Warren
Wene	***WEH**-neh*	Wayne
Wiliama	*WEE-lee-**AH**-muh*	William
Wile	***WEE**-leh*	Willie, Willy

Hawaiian Names

(Most are appropriate for both males and females.)

'Alohilani	*'uh-LOH-hee-LAH-nee*	bright sky
Anuhea	*AH-noo-HEH-uh*	cool, soft fragrance
'Aulani	*'AH⁓oo-LAH-nee*	royal messenger
'Aukai	*'AH⁓oo-KAH⁓ee*	seafarer
Haunani	*HAH⁓oo-NAH-nee*	beautiful dew
Hau'oli	*HAH⁓oo-'OH-lee*	happy
Healoha	*heh-uh-LOH-huh*	a loved one
Hiwahiwa	*HEE-vuh-HEE-vuh*	precious
'Ihilani	*'EE-hee-LAH-nee*	heavenly splendor
'Ilima	*'ee-LEE-muh*	(a yellow flower)
Ipo	*EE-poh*	sweetheart
'Iwalani	*'EE-vuh-LAH-nee*	heavenly seabird
Ka'eo	*kuh-'EH-oh*	the victory
Kahale	*kuh-HAH-leh*	the home
Kahōkū	*kuh-HOH-KOO*	the star
Kaholo	*kuh-HOH-loh*	the runner
Ka'imi	*kuh-'EE-mee*	the search
Kainoa	*kuh-ee-NOH-uh*	the name
Kaipo	*KAH⁓ee-poh*	the sweetheart
Kalā	*kuh-LAH*	the sun
Kālaiwa'a	*KAH-LAH⁓ee-WAH-'ah*	canoe carver
Kalama	*kuh-LAH-muh*	the torch
Kalani	*kuh-LAH-nee*	the heavens
Kaleonahe	*kuh-LEH-oh-NAH-heh*	the soft voice
Kama	*KAH-muh*	child
Kamaka	*kuh-MAH-kuh*	the face
Kamakani	*kuh-muh-KAH-nee*	the wind
Kanani	*kuh-NAH-nee*	the pretty one
Ka'ohe	*kuh-'OH-heh*	the bamboo
Ka'ohu	*kuh-'OH-hoo*	the mist

Kapono	kuh-**POH**-noh	the righteous
Kapua	kuh-**POO**-uh	the blossom
Kauanoe	kuh-OO-uh-**NOH**-eh	the misty rain
Kau'i	**KAH**⁀oo-'ee	the beauty
Kawailani	kuh-**WAH**⁀ee-**LAH**-nee	the heavenly water
Kawena	kuh-**VEH**-nuh	the glow
Keahi	keh-**AH**-hee	the fire
Ke'ala	keh-**'AH**-luh	the fragrance
Kealoha	keh-uh-**LOH**-huh	the beloved
Keawe	keh-**AH**-veh	the strand
Kēhaulani	**KAY**-HAH⁀oo-**LAH**-nee	heavenly dew
Kekai	keh-**KAH**⁀ee	the sea
Kekipi	keh-**KEE**-pee	the rebel
Kekoa	keh-**KOH**-uh	the courageous one
Kekūpa'a	keh-KOO-**PAH**-'ah	the steadfast one
Kele	**KEH**-leh	navigator
Keli'i	keh-**LEE**-'ee	the chief
Keola	keh-**OH**-luh	the life
Kiele	kee-**EH**-leh	gardenia
Ku'uipo	KOO-'oo-**EE**-poh	my sweetheart
Ku'ulei	KOO-'oo-**LEH**⁀ee	my lei, my child
Lanakila	LAH-nuh-**KEE**-luh	victorious
Lani	**LAH**-nee	heaven
Lawai'a	luh-**VAH**⁀ee-'uh	fisherman
Lehua	leh-**HOO**-uh	ōhi'a blossom
Lei	**LEH**⁀ee	flower wreath, child
Leialoha	**LEH**⁀ee-uh-**LOH**-huh	beloved child
Leihulu	**LEH**⁀ee-**HOO**-loo	feather lei
Leilani	**LEH**⁀ee-**LAH**-nee	heavenly child
Leimomi	**LEH**⁀ee-**MOH**-mee	pearl necklace
Leinā'ala	**LEH**⁀ee-NAH-**'AH**-luh	lei of fragrances
Leinani	**LEH**⁀ee-**NAH**-nee	beautiful lei
Leolani	**LEH**-oh-**LAH**-nee	heavenly voice

34

Liko	*LEE*-koh	bud
Lokelani	*LOH*-keh-*LAH*-nee	heavenly rose
Luana	loo-*AH*-nuh	enjoyment
Mahi'ai	*MAH*-hee-*'AH*⁀ee	farmer
Maile	*MAH*⁀ee-leh	myrtle vine
Makamae	*MAH*-kuh-*MAH*⁀eh	precious
Malulani	*MAH*-loo-*LAH*-nee	heavenly calm
Mamo	*MAH*-moh	(a yellow bird)
Manu	*MAH*-noo	bird
Māpuana	*MAH*-poo-*AH*-nuh	wind-blown fragrance
Mele	*MEH*-leh	song, poem
Mililani	*MEE*-lee-*LAH*-nee	heavenly caress
Moana	moh-*AH*-nuh	ocean
Moani	moh-*AH*-nee	fragrance
Mokihana	*MOH*-kee-*HAH*-nuh	(a fragrant plant)
Momi	*MOH*-mee	pearl
Nālani	NAH-*LAH*-nee	the heavens
Nāmaka	NAH-*MAH*-kuh	the eyes
Nani	*NAH*-nee	pretty
Nāpua	NAH-*POO*-uh	the flowers
Noelani	*NOH*-eh-*LAH*-nee	heavenly mist
Nohea	noh-*HEH*-uh	loveliness
Onaona	oh-*NAH*⁀oh-nuh	sweet fragrance
Pi'ilani	*PEE*-'ee-*LAH*-nee	heavenly ascent
Pīkake	*PEE*-*KAH*-keh	jasmine
Pilialoha	*PEE*-lee-uh-*LOH*-huh	beloved relation
Pua	*POO*-uh	flower
Pualani	*POO*-uh-*LAH*-nee	heavenly flower
Puanani	*POO*-uh-*NAH*-nee	pretty flower
Ululani	*OO*-loo-*LAH*-nee	heavenly inspiration
Uluwehi	*OO*-loo-*WEH*-hee	growing in beauty
Wainani	*WAH*⁀ee-*NAH*-nee	beautiful water
Wehilani	*VEH*-hee-*LAH*-nee	heavenly adornment

Social Phrases

By this time, if you've kept in the back of your head the basic rules of the Hawaiian Language, you'll have no difficulty pronouncing all the following phrases — using your knowledge of syllable, sound, and stress. So from this point, you're on your own!

Aloha	Greetings/Farewell
Aloha nō!	Greetings!/Farewell!
Aloha nui loa	Very much love
Aloha kakahiaka	Good morning
Aloha ʻauinalā	Good afternoon
Aloha ahiahi	Good evening
Kala mai iaʻu	Excuse me
ʻO wai kou inoa?	What is your name?
ʻO .... koʻu inoa	My name is ....
Pehea ʻoe?	How are you?
ʻOia mau nō	Same as usual
Pēlā au	So am I
Maikaʻi	Fine
Maikaʻi nō	Very fine
He aha ka mea hou?	What's new?
E ua ana paha	Perhaps it will rain
Pēlā paha, ʻaʻole paha	Maybe so, maybe not
Komo mai	Come in
Nou ka hale	The house is yours
Mai e ʻai	Come and eat
ʻOluʻolu	Please
Mai hilahila!	Don't be bashful!
Mahalo	Thank you
Mahalo nui loa	Thank you very much
He mea iki	Just a trifle/You're welcome
ʻAʻole pilikia	No trouble/You're welcome

Hawaiian	English
Na'u anei keia?	Is this for me?
Pololei/Pololoi	Correct
Nāu wale nō	Just for you
Aloha au iā 'oe	I love you
Me ke aloha	With love
Me ka pumehana	With warmth
Me ka 'oiā'i'o	With sincerity
Aloha 'oe	Farewell to you
Aloha kākou	Aloha to all of us
Ā hui hou kākou	Until we meet again
Hau'oli Lā Hānau	Happy Birthday
Hau'oli Makahiki Hou	Happy New Year
Mele Kalikimaka	Merry Christmas
Mele kākou	Let's sing
Mālama pono!	Be careful!
Minamina	How regrettable
Aloha 'ino!	How unfortunate!
Lawa	Enough
Pau	Finished
Hana hou	Do it again
Mai hele 'oe	Don't go
Noho 'oe	Stay/Sit
Hele	Go ahead
Kipa mai	Come visit
Kipa hou mai!	Come visit again!
Ho'i!	Return!
Kā hea mai	Call me
Hawai'i nei	This Hawai'i, Hawai'i here
Aloha 'āina	Love for the land
Hawai'i aloha	Beloved Hawai'i
Hawai'i Pono'ī	"Hawai'i's Own" (State Anthem)
'Ua mau ke ea ō ka 'āina i ka pono	(State motto)

The life of the land is perpetuated in righteousness

Common Questions

'O wai?	Who?
'O wai 'oe?	Who are you?
Pehea?	How?
Pehea 'oe?	How are you?
Aihea?	Where?
'Auhea 'oe?	Where are you?
He aha?	What?
Nō ke aha?	Why?
I ka wā hea?	When?
Keia?	This?
He aha keia?	What's this?
He aha kēlā?	What's that?
'O wai kēlā?	Who is that?
'Ehia?	How many?
Pono paha?	Is it right?
Hewa paha?	Is it wrong?
He aha ka pilikia?	What's the trouble?
Hola 'ehia keia?	What time is it?
He aha kō makemake?	What do you want?
He aha ke kumu kū'ai?	What's the price?
No hea mai 'oe?	Where are you from originally?
Mai hea mai 'oe?	Where did you come from?
E hele ana 'oe ihea?	Where are you going?
Pehea 'oe e 'ike ai?	How do you know?
'Ehia ou mau makahiki?	How old are you?
'Ua mākaukau anei 'oe?	Are you ready?
'A'ole anei?	Isn't that so?
'A'ole 'oe e 'ike?	You don't know?
Maopopo iā 'oe?	Do you understand?
Pehea la?	What about it?
He aha hou a'e?	What next?

Typical Answers

'Ae	Yes
Hiki	Okay, can do
Maopopo ia'u	I understand
'A'ole maopopo ia'u	I don't understand
'A'ole	No
'A'ole loa	Certainly not
'A'ole hiki	Cannot do
'A'ole pilikia	No trouble
'A'ole ia he mea nui	It's no big thing
'A'ole au e 'ike	I don't know
Pono!	Right!
'Ua pono nō	It is right
Pono nō 'oe!	You're so right!
'A'ole pono	It's not right
'Ua hewa	It is/was wrong
'Ua hewa 'oe	You are/were wrong
'Ua hewa au	I am/was wrong
'A'ole pēlā!	It isn't so!
Pupule kēlā!	That's crazy!
Mai 'ōlelo pēlā	Don't talk like that
Kali	Wait
Kali iki	Wait a little
I keia manawa	At this time, now
Mahope	Later
Pēlā ku'u mana'o	I suppose so
.... o'u mau makahiki	I am .... years old
E hele mai ana au	I'm coming/I will come
E hele aku ana au	I'm going/I will go
Pa'ahana nō au!	I'm busy!
'Ua poina au	I've forgotten
'A'ohe mea	Nothing

Colorful Expressions

'Oia 'ea!	Is that so!
Wela ka hao!	Strike while the iron is hot!
'Auwē!	Oh/Alas!
'Auwī!	Ouch!
'Auwē nō ho'i ē!	Boy-oh-boy!
Ho'olohe!	Listen!
Nānā 'oe!	Look!
Ha'i mai	Tell me
Kōkua mai!	Help!
Mai poina!	Don't forget!
Kāohi mai 'oe!	Hold fast!
Mai molowā	Don't be lazy
Mai maka'u	Don't be afraid
Maka'u au	I'm afraid
Hele mai	Come here
Hele aku!	Go away/Beat it!
'Āwīwī!	Be quick!
E aho ia	That's better
Māluhiluhi au	I'm tired
Hele a hiamoe	Go to bed
'Ua pō'ele'ele	It's dark
Pōloli au	I'm hungry
Make wai au	I'm thirsty
'Ua ma'i au	I'm sick
'Ua 'eha ia'u	I'm hurt
'Ua mehameha au	I'm lonely
Pa'akikī!	Stubborn/Difficult!
Kulikuli!	Shut up!
Lapuwale!	Good-for-nothing!
Hūpō!	Fool!
Lōlō!	Stupid!

Pupule!	Crazy!
'Ōpulepule	Kind of crazy
Kāpulu!	Sloppy!
Pelapela!	Filthy!
Pupuka!	Ugly!
Pilau!	Putrid/Rotten/Stink!
Huhū	Anger
Huhū wela loa	Very hot anger
Ho'okano	Conceited
Ho'opaumanawa	Waste time
Hoihoi	Interesting
'Ē!	Hey!
Hui!	Yoo-hoo!
Eia nei!	You there!
He wahine u'i	A beautiful woman
He kanaka ikaika	A powerful person
He kanaka pono 'oe	You're an honest person
Akamai 'oe	You're smart
Lokomaika'i 'oe	You're good-hearted
'Ōpiopio loa 'oe	You're so young
Ho'omalimali	To flatter, flattery
He mea nui ia	An important thing
He mea waiwai loa	A very valuable thing
Ho'omanawanui	Be patient
Imua	Forward, progress
Hana hou	Do it again
Ha'ina 'ia mai ana ka puana	Tell the refrain (theme of the song)
Pau!	Finished!
Kōlea	Pacific golden plover (carpetbagger)
'Emi	Cheap
Pipi'i	Expensive
Pohō	Out-of-luck

41

Everyday Terms

'a'ā	stony, rough lava
'a'ala	fragrance, perfume
aikāne	intimate (male) friend
'āina	land
akamai	smart
ala	path
alanui	street, road
ali'i	chief
aloha	love, affection, pity, mercy, compassion, greetings, farewell
anu	cool, cold, to have a cold
'au	to swim, travel by sea
'au'au	to bathe
'elemakule	elderly man
hae	flag
hala	pandanus tree
hālau	canoe long house, hula school
hale	house, building
hale 'aina	restaurant
hale keaka	theater
hale leka	post office
hale ma'i, hakupila	hospital
hale moe, hokele	hotel
hale pa'ahao	jail, prison
hale pāpa'i	apartment building, condominium
hale pule	church
hana	work
hānai	to adopt, adopted
haole	foreigner, Caucasian person

hapa	half, part
hāpai	pregnant, to carry
hau'oli	happy
Hawai'i	largest Hawaiian island; Hawaiian
he'e nalu	to surf, surfing
heiau	ancient religious enclosure
hele	to go
hikie'e	large Hawaiian couch
hilahila	shyness, embarrassment
hoe	a paddle, to paddle
holo	run, ride, sail
holokū	a gown with train
honi	kiss
ho'olaule'a	celebration
ho'omalimali	to flatter, flattery
hou	again, new, fresh
huhū	anger
hui	group, club, to join
hu'i	ache, throb
huki	to pull
hukilau	community net fishing
hula	Hawaiian dance
'ili'ili	beach pebbles, stone castanets
ikaika	strong, powerful
'ike	to know, see
iki	small, little
'īlio	dog
'imi loa	search, seeker
imu	earth oven
inoa	name
'iole	rat, mouse
ipo	sweetheart

ipu	gourd, drum
ipukukui	lamp
ka'a	car
kahiki	foreign country; Tahiti
kahiko	old, ancient
kāhili	feather standard of royalty
Kaho'olawe	eighth largest Hawaiian Island
kahuna	ancient Hawaiian expert, advisor, and practitioner
kālā	money, dollar
kālua	to bake
kama'āina	native born person, local resident
kanaka	human
kāne	male, husband
kapa	tapa cloth, clothing, blanket
kapakahi	uneven, crooked
kapu	sacred, forbidden
Kaua'i	fourth largest Hawaiian island
kauka	doctor
kaukau	"chow" (slang)
kaulana	famous
kaumaha	unhappy
keiki	baby, child
kelepona	telephone
kiawe	algaroba tree
ki'i	statue (tiki), image, picture
ki'i 'oni'oni	moving picture, movie
kinipōpō	ball
kipuka	contrastive area in environment
koa	courageous soldier; acacia tree
kōkua	aid, help
kolohe	rascal

kona	leeward side of an island
koʻolau	windward side of an island
kukui	candlenut (State) tree; lamp, light
kula	open country; gold; school
kula kiʻekiʻe	high school
kula nui	university
kuleana	private property, responsibility
kuli	deaf; knee
kumu	source, teacher
lā	sun, day
lāʻau	tree, plant, stick, club, wood, forest, medicine
lāhui	race, nation
lānai	veranda
Lānaʻi	sixth largest Hawaiian island
lani	sky, heaven
lau hala	pandanus leaf (used in plaiting)
lei	wreath, garland of flowers
leka	letter
lele	jump, leap, fly
liʻi, liʻiliʻi	small, tiny
lio	horse
loa	long, much, very
lohi	slow, late, tardy
lōʻihi	tall, height
lomilomi	massage
lua	two; pit, toilet
luahine	elderly woman
lūʻau	feast
luna	boss
mahalo	thank you
mahope	after, later, behind

mai	hither, toward the speaker; don't
ma'i	sick
makai	toward the sea
māka'i	policeman
makana	gift
make	to die, dead
makemake	to want, to like, desire
malihini	newcomer
malo	loincloth
maluhia	peace, quiet
māmalu	umbrella
mana	spiritual power
manō	shark
manuahi	free, no charge
Maui	second largest Hawaiian island
mauka	inland, upland
mea he'e nalu	surfer
mele	song, poem, to sing
menehune	Hawaiian elf
moe	sleep, lie down
moe 'uhane	dream
moku	separation, district, island, ship
mokulele	airplane
Moloka'i	fifth largest Hawaiian island
momona	fertile, fat
mo'o	reptile, lizard
mo'olelo	story
mu'umu'u	loose gown
nalu	wave, surf
nane	riddle
nani	beauty, pretty
nei	this place, here

Nēnē	Hawaiian goose, official 50th State bird
Ni'ihau	seventh largest Hawaiian island
noho	to live, to dwell, to sit, chair
nui	big, important, many
O'ahu	third largest Hawaiian island
'oe	you (singular)
'oi	superior, sharp, best
'ōkolehao	ti-root liquor
ola	life, health
'ōlelo	language, speech, to talk
oli	chant
onaona	fragrance, perfume
'ono	delicious
'ōpiopio	young
'ōpū	stomach
pā	enclosure, wall, fence, lot
Pā'ele	Negro, black
pāhoehoe	smooth lava
pahu	drum, box, keg, barrel
paka	tobacco
Pākē	Chinese
palaka	checked print cloth
palapala	document
pali	cliff
pānini	cactus
paniolo	cowboy
papa he'e nalu	surfboard
pau	finished
pā'ū	sarong
pī	stingy
pilikia	trouble

po'e	people
pōmaika'i	blessing, good luck, fortunate
ponimō'ī	carnation
pōpoki	cat
pū'ili	split bamboo rattles
puka	perforation, hole, door
puke	book
pulu	wet; tree fern down
pumehana	warm
pūne'e	couch, single bed
pūpū	shell, appetizer
u'i	beautiful, youthful
'uku	flea
'ukulele	four string Hawaiian musical instrument
'ulī'ulī	gourd rattle
'umeke	calabash
uwē	cry, weep, lament
wa'a	canoe
wahine	female, wife
waiwai	rich
wela	hot
wikiwiki	hurry, quick

The standard references used for the spelling and pronunciation of Hawaiian terms are the **Hawaiian Dictionary** (Revised Edition, 1971) by Mary Kawena Pūku'i and Samuel H. Elbert, and **Place Names Of Hawai'i** (Revised and Expanded, 1974) by Mrs. Pūku'i, Dr. Elbert, and Esther T. Mo'okini. Both books are published by the University Press of Hawai'i. Always consult these comprehensive sources.